To Larry and Viv Scott
to refresh memories of your travels
fondly
Harry + Ruth Kemnitz Freund

MILT KEMNITZ

KEMNITZ

Door Knocker · Durham Cathedral

LONDON
AND BACK

Marble Arch · Hyde Park · London

KEMNITZ

A book of personal drawings
by **MILT KEMNITZ**

Produced and Edited by
E. L. KEMNITZ

Published by
M. N. and E. L. KEMNITZ
BOX 7390
ANN ARBOR, MICHIGAN 48107

KRAWITZ

Heathrow Airport - London

London's Post Office Tower

KEMNITZ

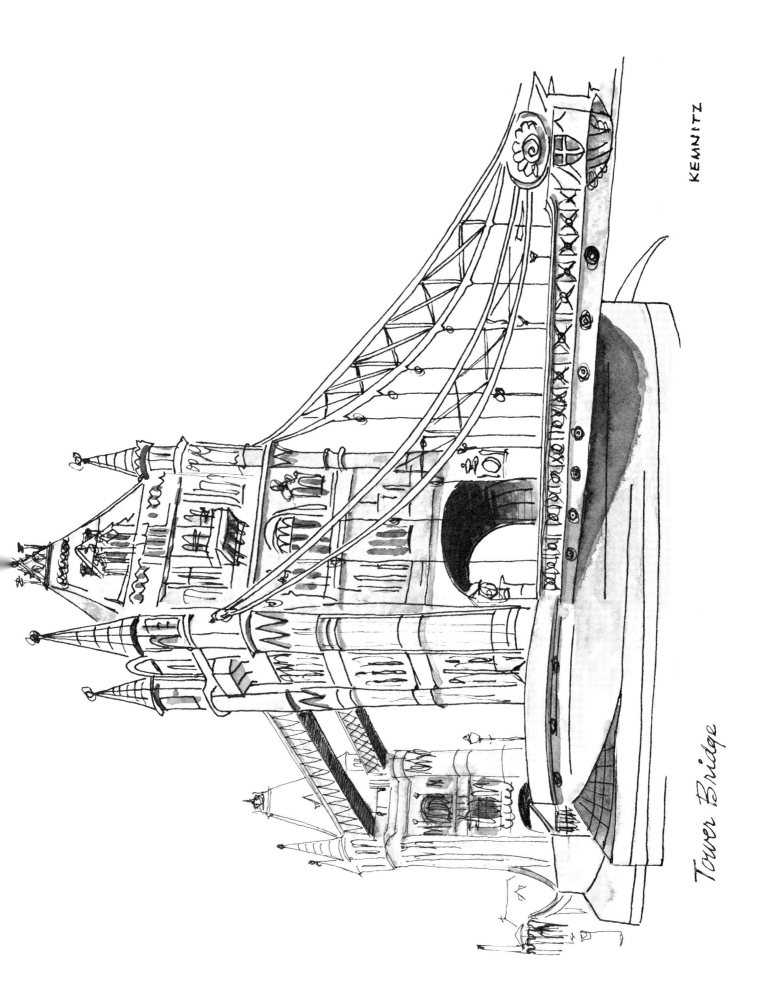

Tower Bridge

KEMNITZ

Southwark Cathedral - London

KEMNITZ

St. Paul's

KEMNITZ

The Fleet Street Griffin

KEMNITZ

Law Courts, the Strand, London

KEMNITZ

ART OF ISLAM

The British Museum

KEMNITZ

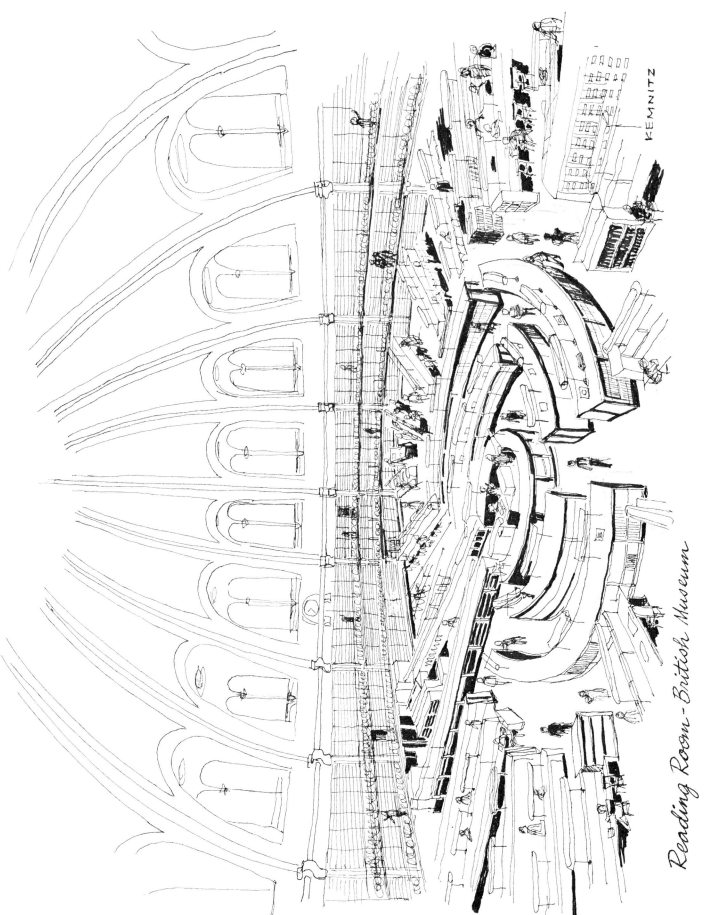

Reading Room - British Museum

KEMNITZ

WM.
YOUNGER

WHEATSHEAF

SCOTCH
ALES

KEMNITZ

16th Century Carved Wooden Ark
The Jewish Museum - London

KEMNITZ

Hotel Russell - Russell Square - London

KEMNITZ

In Oxford Street - London

KEMNITZ

EGLISE PROTESTANTE FRANCAISE DE LONDRES

KING EDWARD VI
1550 ASYLUM TO
HUGUENOTS

EGLISE
INVITATION
CORDIALE
A TOUS

ESPANOL
POLISH
ESPERANTO

KEMNITZ

French Church in Soho Square, London

Donkey's Years at the Globe

Opera and St. Martin's

KEMNITZ

...tin-in-the Fields from the Porch of the National Gallery

KEM

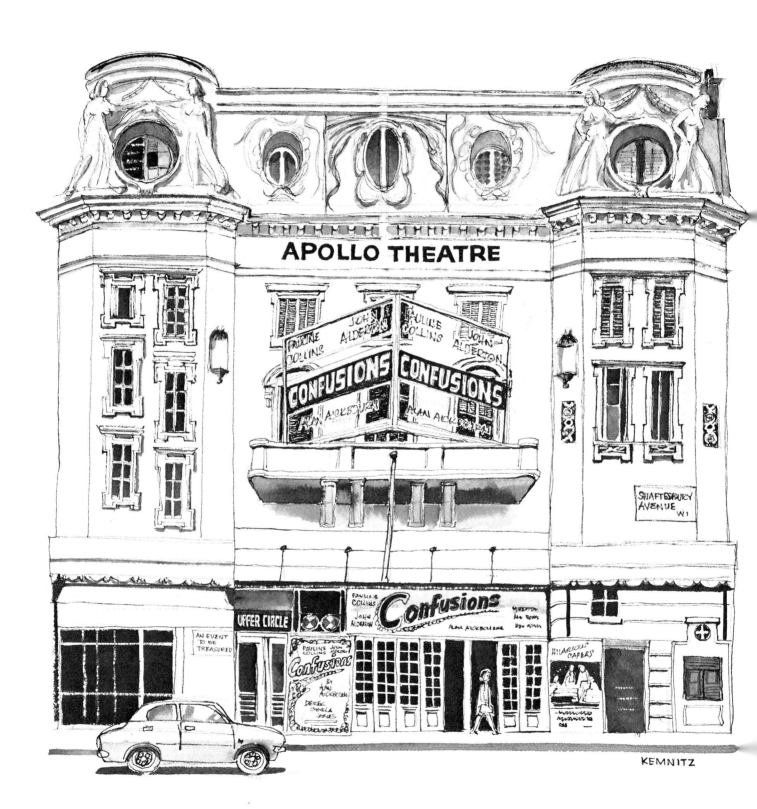

Hippodrome

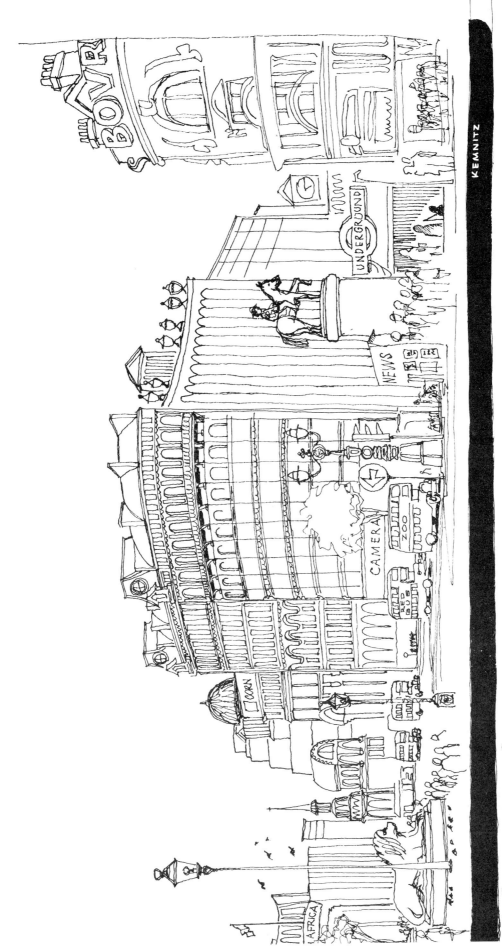

Trafalgar Square

KEMNITZ

Piccadilly Circus Fountain

KEMNITZ

Westminster Abbey

Westminster Schoolyard – London

KEMNITZ

KEMNITZ

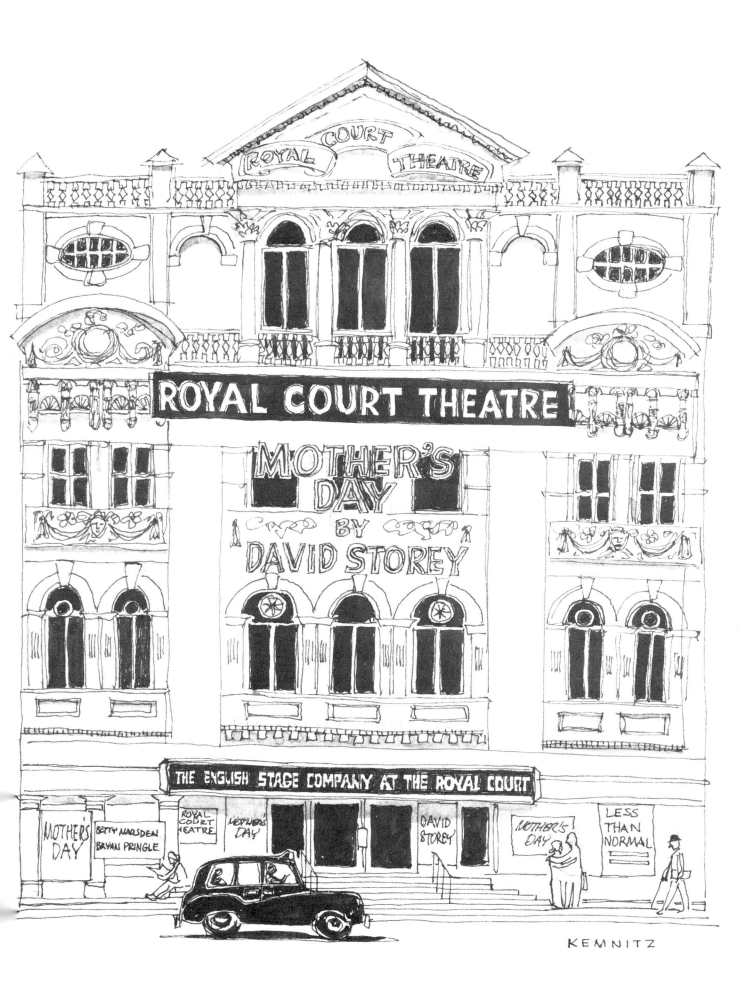

PIZZ
REST

Ukranian Cathedral

KEMNITZ

The London Oratory - Brompton

KEMNITZ

Iolanthe House built in 1883 by Sir William Gilbert of Gilbert and Sullivan

KEMNITZ

Harrods, London

KEMNITZ

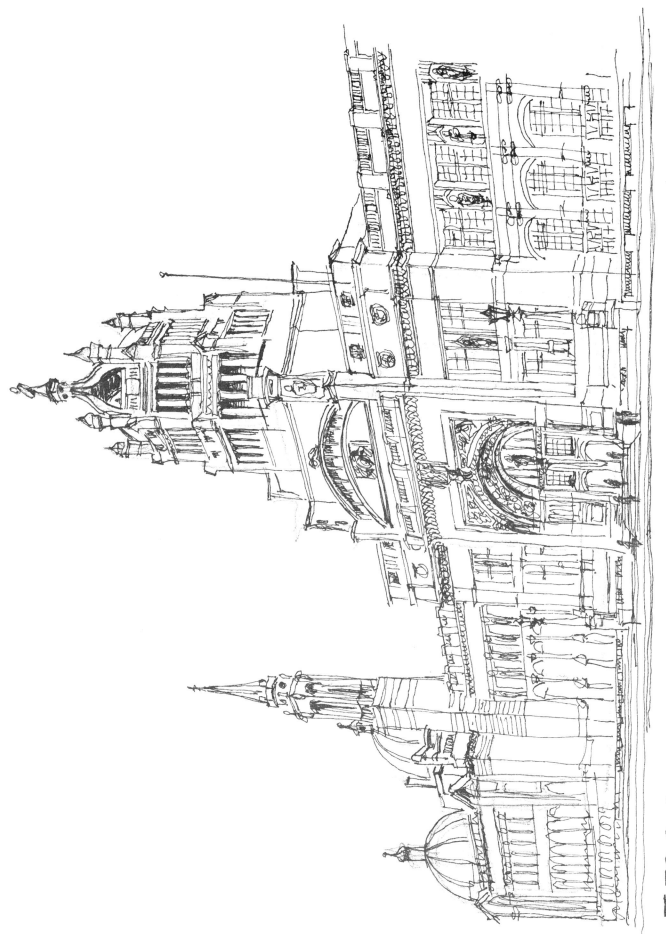

V&A. The Victoria and Albert Museum
Exhibition Road and Cromwell Road

KEMNITZ

KEMNITZ

Museum of Natural History 1881

The Albert Memorial

KEMNITZ

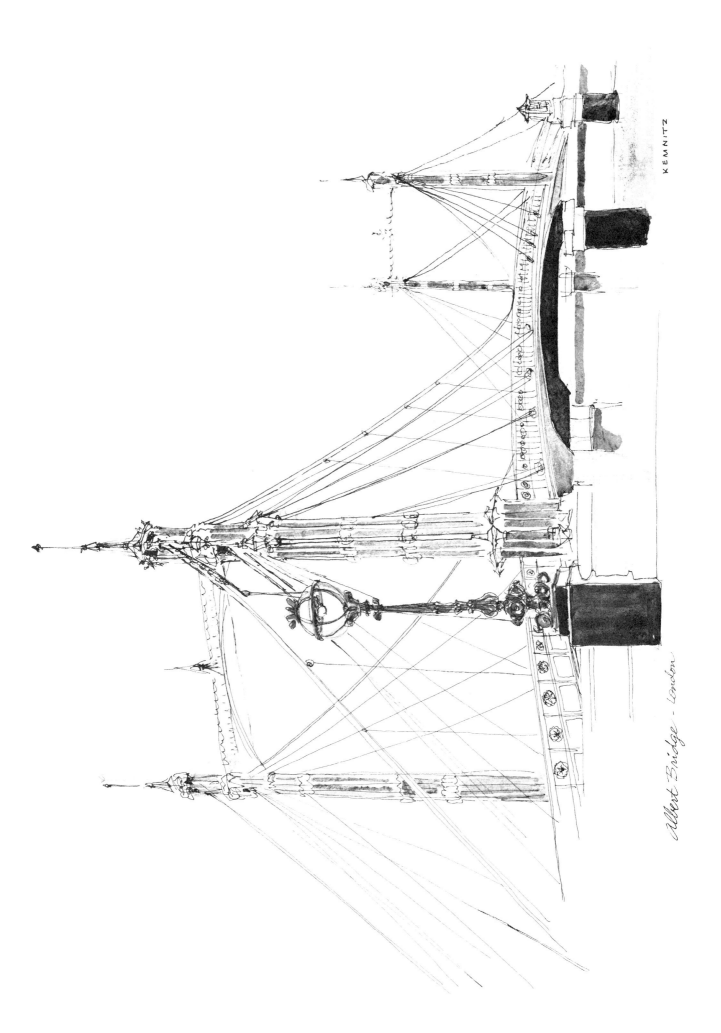

Albert Bridge - London

KEMNITZ

Smith Square - London

KEMNITZ

TATE
GALLERY

TATE
GALLERY

RED BUS

UNDERGROUND

JOHN
CONSTABLE
1776-1837
Exhibition

KEMNITZ

KEMNITZ

Hyde Park Fountain
London

VICTORIA

NEWS

TRAVEL KODAK

KEMNITZ

Windsor House

London's Portobello Road

KEMNITZ

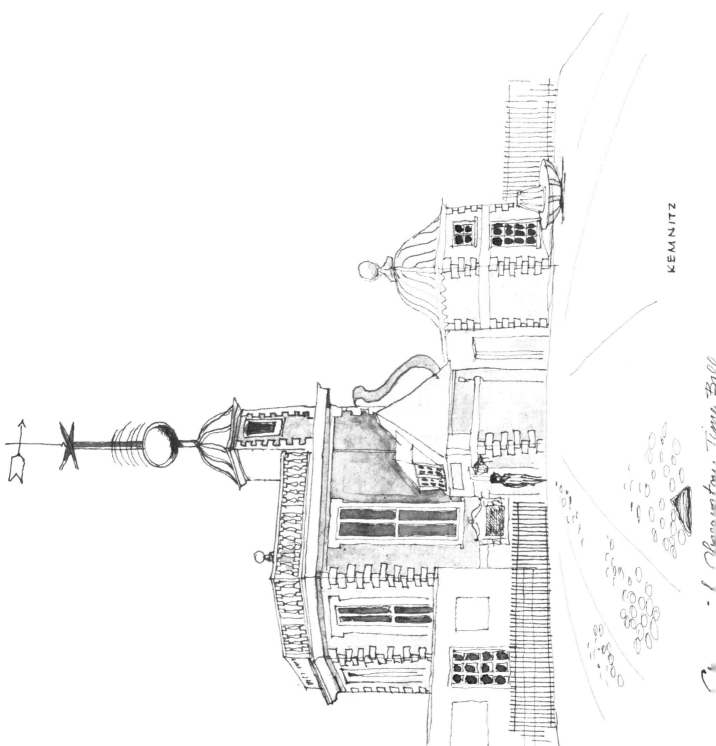

KEMNITZ

Cutty Sark at Greenwich

KEMNITZ

KEMNITZ

LISA
OF
LAMBETH

LONDON ROAD - LEWES LINE

KING'S CROSS STATION

WATERLOO STATION

1914

1918

VICTORIA

LONDON

NEAR RYE IN SUSSEX

ETCHINGHAM

State Express

FINLAYS   FINLAYS

BRIGHTON

KEMNITZ

Victoria

KEMNITZ

Victoria Station - London

KEMNITZ

Sea Front - Brighton

KEMNITZ

The Lift · Brighton Sea Front

Palace Pier, Brighton

KEMNITZ

West Pier, Brighton

KEMNITZ

AMUSEMENTS

BINGO

WEST PIER

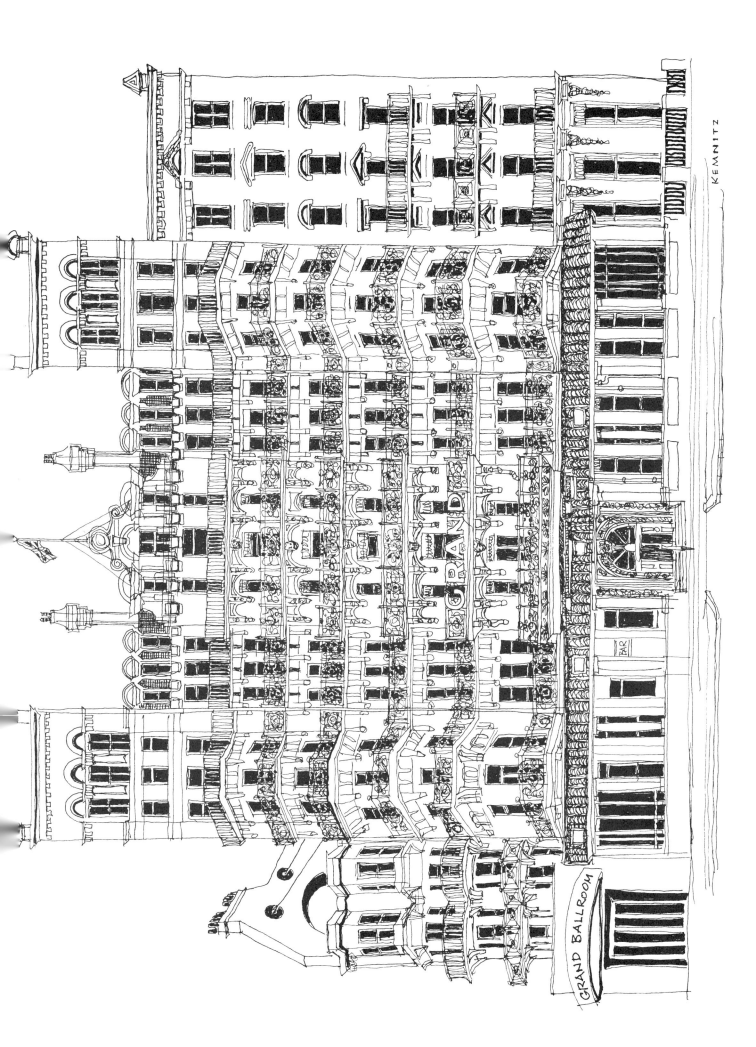

GRAND BALLROOM

BAR

GRAND

KEMNITZ

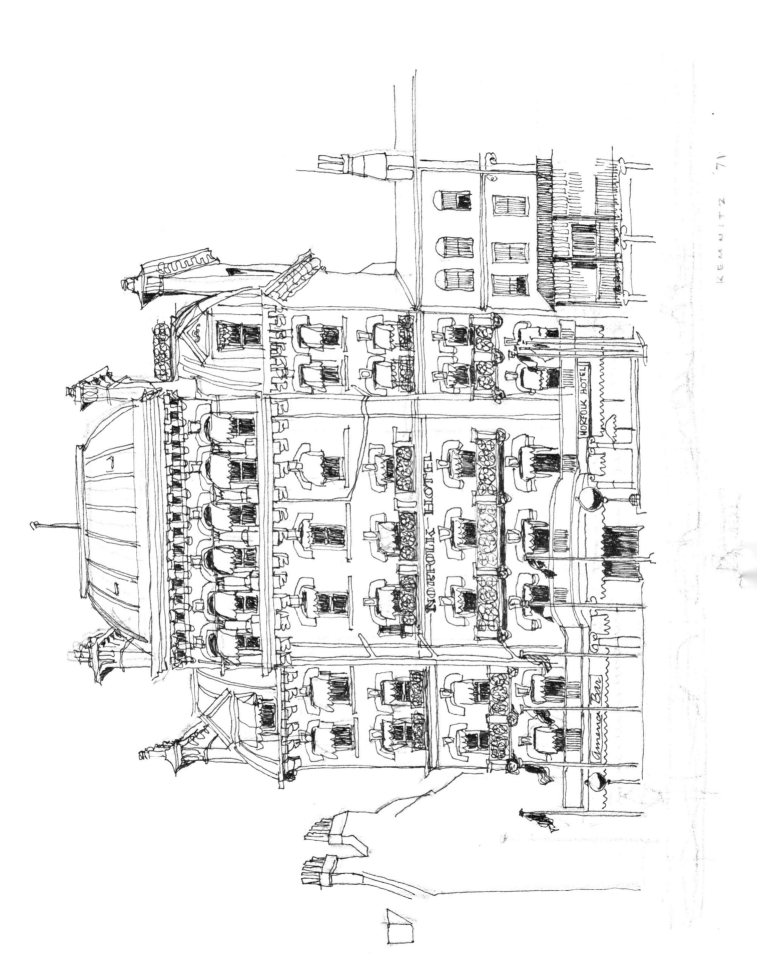

NORFOLK HOTEL

NORFOLK HOTEL

KEMNITZ '71

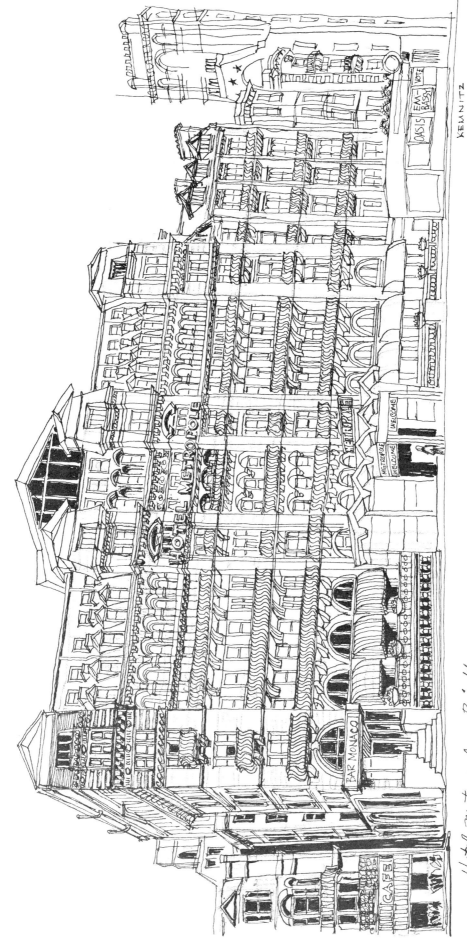

Hotel Metropole - Brighton

KEMNITZ

Hotel Victoria, Brighton

KEMNITZ

KEMNITZ

Clock tower - Brighton

KEMNITZ

27/170   Royal Pavilion - Brighton

KEMNITZ

THE LANES BRIGHTON

Sloopy's Discotheque · Brighton

Brighton Movie House

KEMNITZ

University of Sussex

KEMNITZ

Preston Manor – Brighton

KEMNITZ

Viaduct in Brighton

KEMNITZ

50/70

Lewes Crescent - Brighton

KEMNITZ

View Toward the Sea
from 36 Sussex Square

KEMNITZ

Brighton

KEMNITZ

VIEW TOWARD THE DOWNS ~ Brighton
FROM 36 SUSSEX SQUARE

KEMP TOWN TUNNEL
THROUGH CHALK DOWNS
AT BRIGHTON FREIGHT
YARDS

KEMNITZ

Along Boundary Road · Hove

KEMNITZ

MEALS ANYTIME

AT BRIGHTON STATION

KEMNITZ

RYE, SUSSEX MAY 29, 1971

KEMNITZ

KEMNITZ

Rye Church

St. Mary's
Church in Rye

KEMNITZ

14th Century Gate House
Michelham Priory

KEMNITZ

The Wichelham Priory, Sussex, founded 1229
Owned by the Sackville Family 1603–1897

KEMNITZ

At Sissinghurst Castle
The Tower and the hops drying ovens
Home of V. Sackville-West and Harold Nicholson

KEMNITZ

Arundel

KEMNITZ

SHEFFIELD PARK

BLUEBELL

328

KEMNITZ

Steam Museum &
Railroad

STEAM AT
BLUEBELL RAILWAY
SHEFFIELD PARK
SUSSEX

BIRCH GROVE
BUILT 1898 AT BRIGHTON

THE BLUE CIRCLE   2-2-0 FLYWHEEL
1860-70 DESIGN   BUILT 1926

KEMNITZ

KEMNITZ

Chichester
Cross
built about 1500

Chichester Cathedral

KEMNITZ

Chichester Festival Theatre
act in Sheridan's "Rivals"

KEMNITZ

KEMNITZ

Winchester Cathedral

Salisbury Cathedral

KEMNITZ

The Abbey at Bath

KEMNITZ

Roman baths in Bath, Somerset

KEMNITZ

BEACH AT SWANSEA, WALES

KEMNITZ

Finn Barre Cathedral Cork, Ireland

KEMNITZ

*Ireland's Blarney Castle
with the Blarney Stone*

KEMNITZ

9th Century Norman Tower
Kildare, Ireland

KEMNITZ

Campanile, Trinity College, Dublin

KEMNITZ

Unitarian Church · Dublin

KEMNITZ

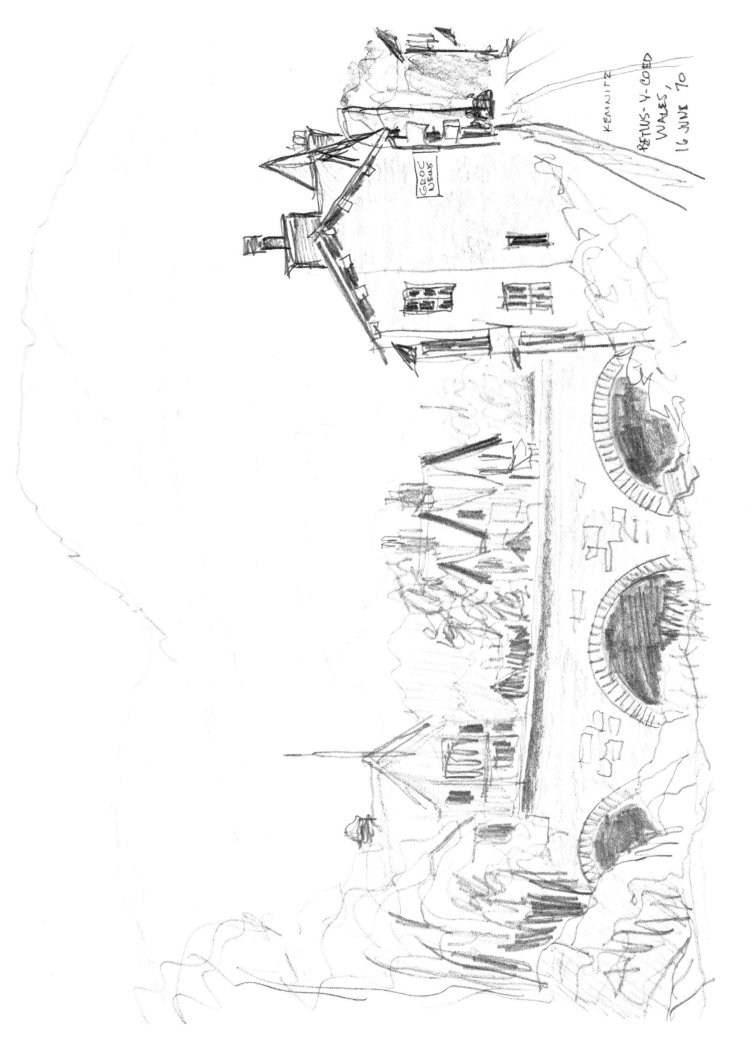

KEMNITZ

Coventry Cathedral

COVENTRY CATHEDRAL

KEMNITZ

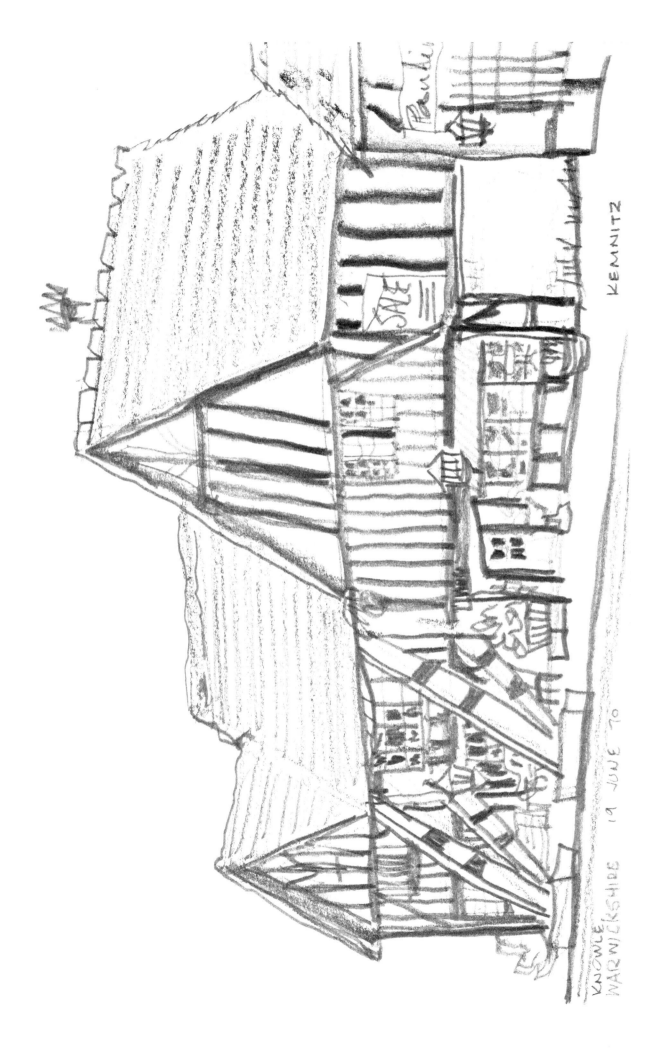

KNOWLE
WARWICKSHIRE   19 JUNE 70

KEMNITZ

KEMNITZ

Edinburgh - High Street

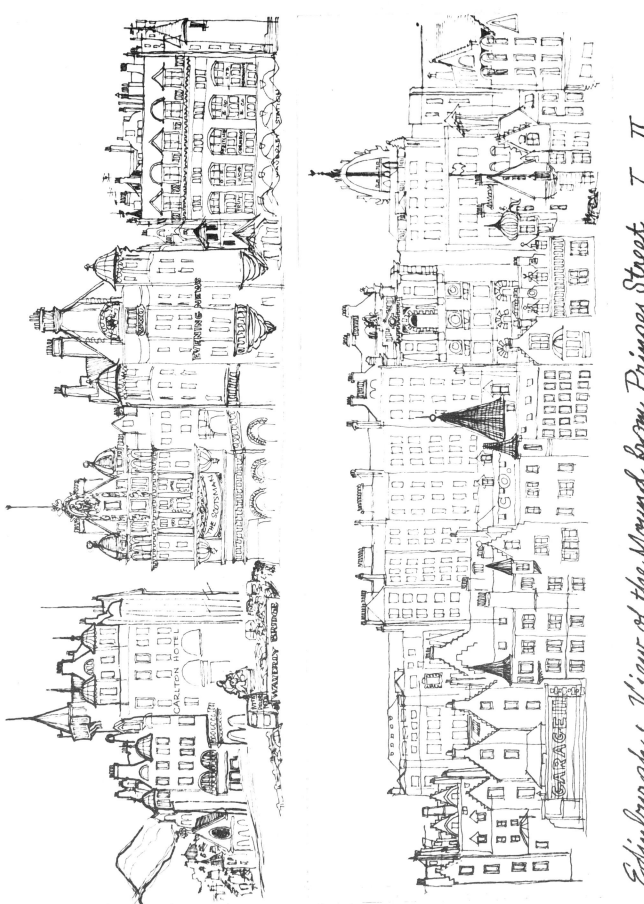

Edinburgh ' View of the Mound from Princes Street I , II

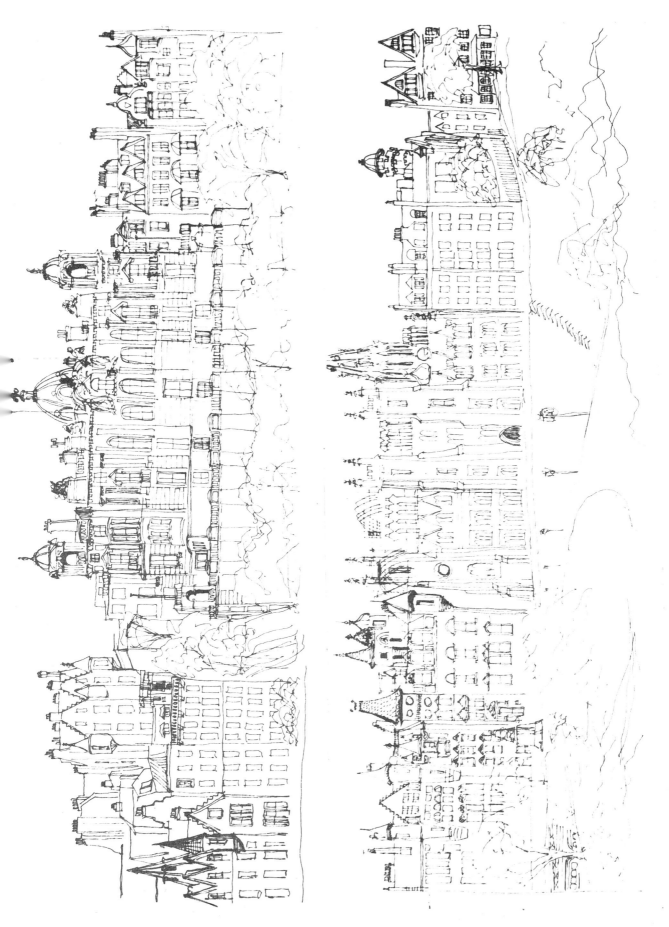

Edinburgh · View of the Mound from Princes Street III, IV

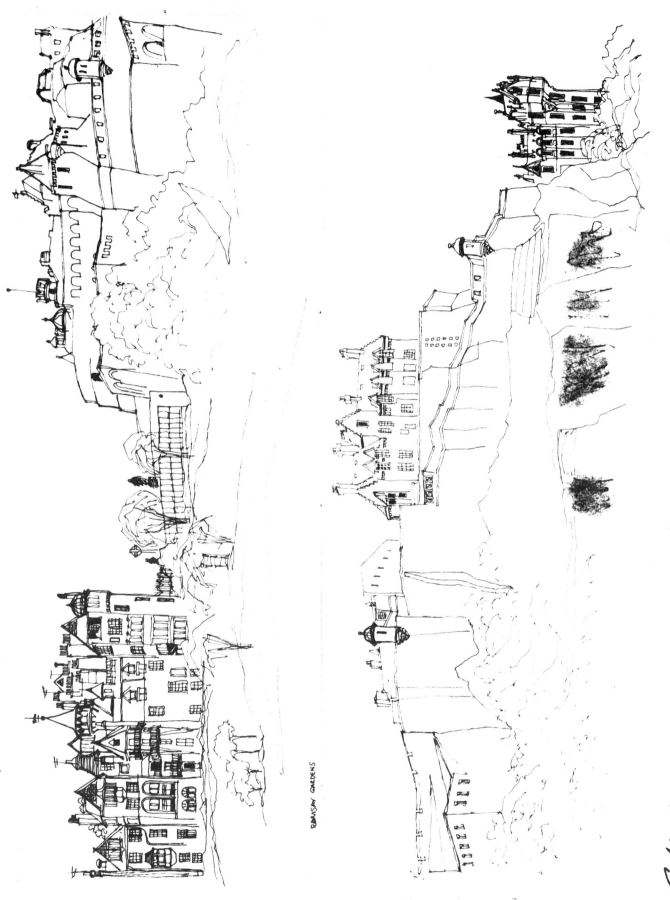

RAMSAY GARDENS

Edinburgh · View of the Mound from Princes Street   I, II

Durham Cathedral

KEMNITZ

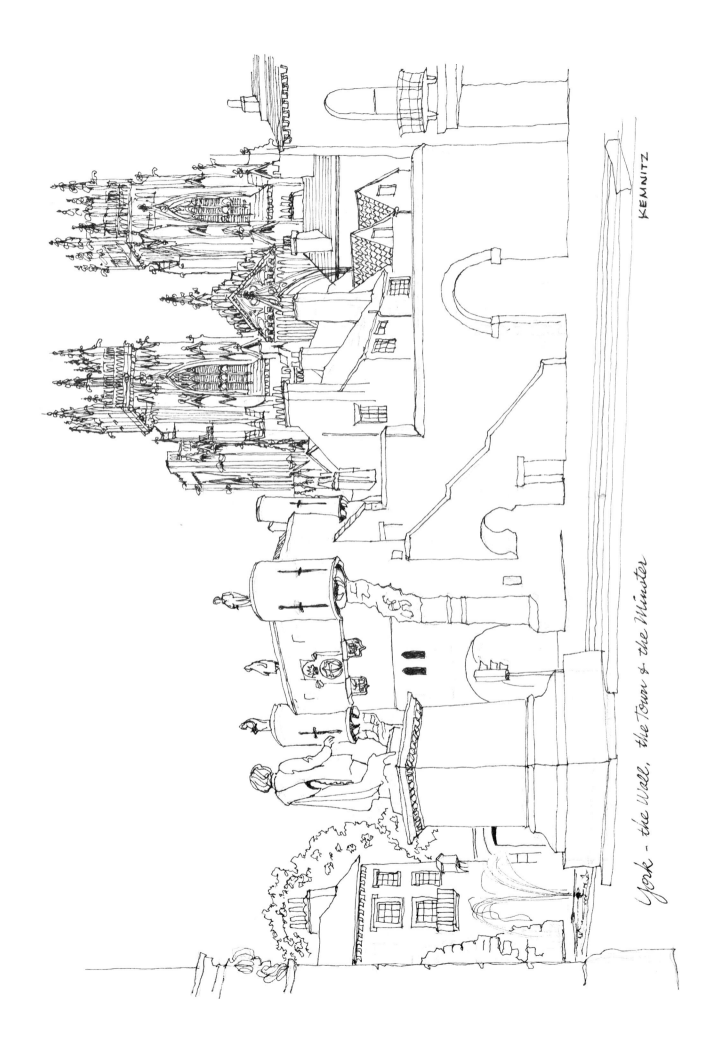

York - the Wall, the Town & the Minster

KEMNITZ

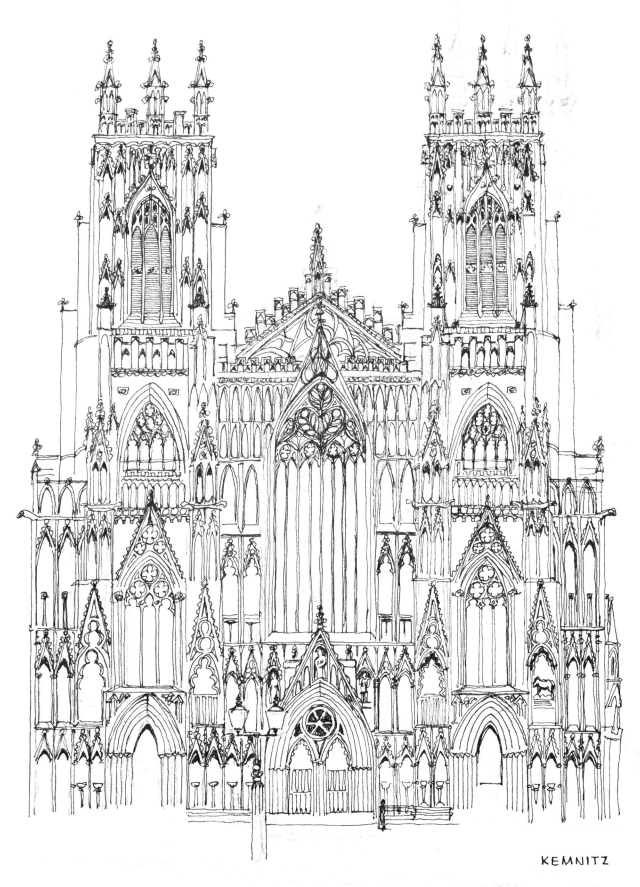

KEMNITZ

York Minster

Ely Cathedral - West Tower

KEMNITZ

Ely Cathedral – Octagon and Lantern

KEMNITZ

behind the Cathedral

KEMNITZ

street in an English University town   KEMNITZ

KEMNITZ

King's College, Cambridge

Sir Christopher Wren's Building, Emmanuel College, Cambridge

KEMNITZ

KEMNITZ

Punting on the Cam

Queen's College wooden bridge, Cambridge

KEMNITZ

Tom Tower, Christ Church Oxford 1671 (Wren)

KEMNITZ

BODLEIAN

Entrance to Bodleian Library, Oxford

KEMNITZ

Sheldonian Theatre, Oxford

KEMNITZ

KEMNITZ

Oxford's Radcliffe Camera

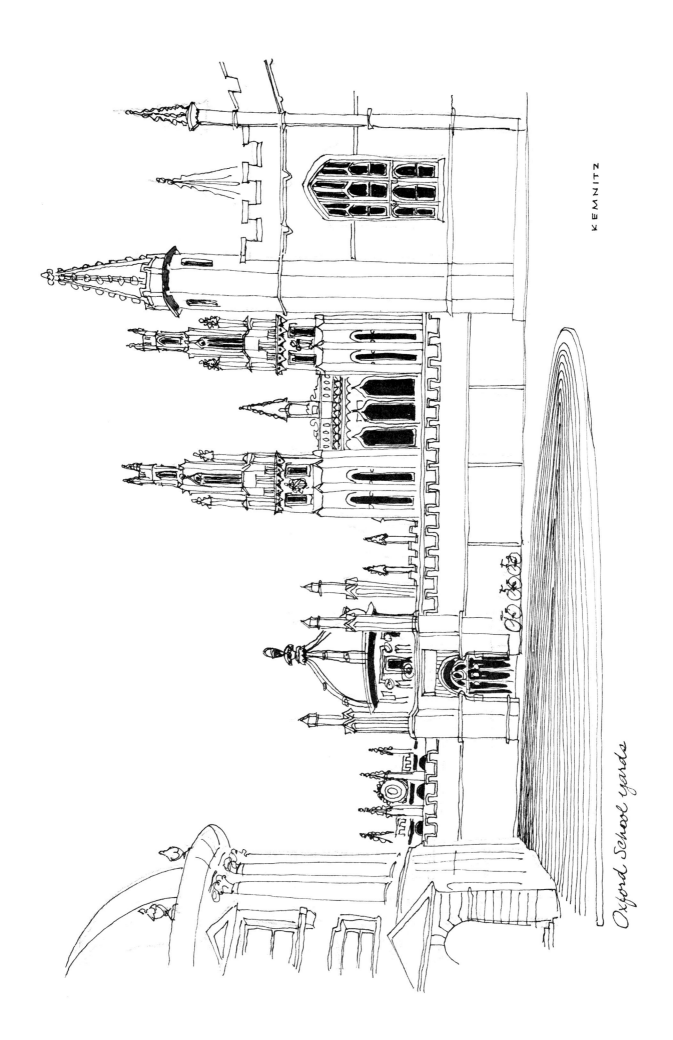

Oxford School yard

KEMNITZ

Canterbury Cathedral

KEMNITZ

Heathrow Airport Departures

KEMNITZ

KEMNITZ